KETO

COOKBOOK

KETOGENIC RECIPES TO BOOST YOUR METABOLISM AND INCREASE FAT BURNING

[EMILY STEVENSON]

Text Copyright © [EMILY STEVENSON]

Legal & Disclaimer

The information contained in this book and its contents is not designed to replace or take the place of any form of medical or professional advice; and is not meant to replace the need for independent medical, financial, legal or other professional advice or services, as may be required. The content and information in this book has been provided for educational and entertainment purposes only.

The content and information contained in this book has been compiled from sources deemed reliable, and it is accurate to the best of the Author's knowledge, information and belief. However, the Author cannot guarantee its accuracy and validity and cannot be held liable for any errors and/or omissions. Further, changes are periodically made to this book as and when needed. Where appropriate and/or necessary, you must consult a professional (including but not limited to your doctor, attorney, financial advisor or such other professional advisor) before using any of the suggested remedies, techniques, or information in this book.

Upon using the contents and information contained in this book, you agree to hold harmless the Author from and against any damages, costs, and expenses, including any legal fees potentially resulting from the application of any of the information provided by this book. This disclaimer applies to any loss, damages or injury caused by the use and application, whether directly or indirectly, of any advice or information presented, whether for breach of contract, tort, negligence, personal injury, criminal intent, or under any other cause of action.

You agree to accept all risks of using the information presented inside this book.

You agree that by continuing to read this book, where appropriate and/or necessary, you shall consult a professional (including but not limited to your doctor, attorney, or financial advisor or such other advisor as needed) before using any of the suggested remedies, techniques, or information in this book.

TABLE OF CONTENTS

KETO DINNER RECIPES 89

INTRODUCTION

Thank you for purchasing the book *'Keto Cookbook'*.

A keto or ketogenic diet is a low-carb, moderate protein, higher-fat diet that can help you burn fat more effectively. It has many benefits for weight loss, health, and performance, as shown in over 50 studies.

1

That's why it's recommended by a growing number of doctors and healthcare practitioners.

2

A keto diet is especially useful for losing excess body fat, reducing hunger, and improving type 2 diabetes or metabolic syndrome.

3

Here, you'll learn how to eat a keto diet based on real foods.

CONVERSION TABLES

Cooking Volume Measurement Conversion Chart				
Cup	**Fluid oz**	**Tablespoon**	**Teaspoon**	**Milliliter**
1 cup	8 oz	16 Tbsp	48 tsp	237 ml
¾ cup	6 oz	12 Tbsp	36 tsp	177 ml
$^2/_3$ cup	5 oz	11 Tbsp	32 tsp	158 ml
½ cup	4 oz	8 Tbsp	24 tsp	118 ml
$^1/_3$ cup	3 oz	5 Tbsp	16 tsp	79 ml
¼ cup	2 oz	4 Tbsp	12 tsp	59 ml
$^1/_8$ cup	1 oz	2 Tbsp	6 tsp	30 ml
$^1/_{16}$ cup	.5 oz	1 Tbsp	3 tsp	15 ml

Temperature Conversions

Fahrenheit	Celsius	Gas Mark	Description
225	107	1/4	Very Low
250	121	1/2	Very Low
275	135	1	Low
300	149	2	Low
325	163	3	Moderate
350	177	4	Moderate
375	190	5	Moderately Hot
400	204	6	Moderately Hot
425	218	7	Hot
450	238	8	Hot
475	246	9	Very Hot

Pounds to Kilograms conversion table

Pounds (lb)	Kilograms (kg)	Kilograms+Grams (kg+g)
1 lb	0.454 kg	0 kg 454 g
2 lb	0.907 kg	0 kg 907 g
3 lb	1.361 kg	1 kg 361 g
4 lb	1.814 kg	1 kg 814 g

KETO BREAKFAST RECIPES

1. DELICIOUS COCONUT FLOUR WAFFLES

Prep.Time: 10 min - **Cooking Time:** 15 min - **Servings:** 5

Ingredients:

- ✓ 4 tbsp. coconut flour
- ✓ 5 eggs, separated by white and yolk
- ✓ 1 tsp. baking powder
- ✓ 4-5 tbsp. granulated stevia or your own sweetener
- ✓ 3 tbsp. whole milk
- ✓ 1 tsp. vanilla
- ✓ 4½ oz. butter, melted

Directions:

1. Whisk the egg whites in a bowl until they form stiff peaks.
2. In another bowl, mix the egg yolk with the coconut flour, the stevia or sweetener, and the baking powder.
3. Add the melted butter. Do so slowly, mixing until the batter is smooth.
4. Add the milk and the vanilla.
5. Combine the mixture of the first bowl with the second one, folding it in to keep the fluffiness of the batter.
6. When the waffle maker is warmed up, pour in some waffle mixture. When it is golden brown, it's finished. Repeat until all the batter is used.

Nutrition: calories 277 – Fat 22– Carbs 4.3 - Protein 8

2. BROWNIE MUFFINS FOR KETOHEADS

Prep.Time: 15 min - **Cooking Time:** 15 min - **Servings:** 6

Ingredients:

- ✓ 1 cup golden flaxseed meal
- ✓ 1 tbsp. cinnamon
- ✓ ¼ cup cocoa powder
- ✓ ½ tsp. salt
- ✓ ½ tsp. baking powder
- ✓ 1 egg
- ✓ 2 tbsp. coconut oil
- ✓ ¼ cup sugar-free caramel syrup
- ✓ ½ cup pumpkin purée
- ✓ 1 tbsp. vanilla extract
- ✓ 1 tbsp. apple cider vinegar
- ✓ ¼ cup slivered almonds

Directions:

1. Preheat oven to 350°F.
2. Place all the ingredients except the almonds into a large mixing bowl, and combine well.
3. In a lined muffin pan, fill each space, dividing the batter into 6 parts.
4. Sprinkle the almonds on top.
5. Bake for around 15 minutes

Nutrition: calories 185 – Fat 13.5 - Carbs 3.5 - Protein 7.4

3. KETO CHEDDAR AND SAGE WAFFLE

Prep.Time: 10 min - **Cooking Time:** 10 minutes - **Servings**: 12

Ingredients:

- ✓ 1⅓ cups coconut flour
- ✓ 3 tbsp. baking powder
- ✓ 1 tsp. ground sage, dried
- ✓ ½ tsp. salt
- ✓ ¼ tsp. garlic powder
- ✓ 2 cups canned coconut milk
- ✓ ½ cup water
- ✓ 2 eggs
- ✓ 3 tbsp. coconut oil, melted
- ✓ 1 cup cheddar cheese, shredded

Directions:

1. Mix the flour, baking powder and seasonings together in a bowl.
2. Add the coconut milk, water and coconut oil and beat them until they form a stiff batter.
3. Combine with the cheese.
4. Grease and heat the waffle iron, and pour onto each iron section⅓ cup of the batter.
5. Close the iron until the waffles are browned

Nutrition: calories 214 – Fat 17.2-Carbs 3.8 - Protein 6.5

4. KETO CASSEROLE FOR BREAKFAST

Prep.Time: 20 min - **Cooking Time:**60 min -
Servings:8

Ingredients:

- ✓ ¼ cup flaxseed meal
- ✓ 1 cup almond flour
- ✓ 10 eggs
- ✓ 1 lb. breakfast sausage
- ✓ 4 oz. cheese
- ✓ 6 tbsp. light maple syrup
- ✓ 4 tbsp. butter
- ✓ ½ tsp. onion powder
- ✓ ½ tsp. garlic powder
- ✓ ¼ tsp. sage
- ✓ Salt and pepper

Directions:

1. In a pan on medium heat, add the breakfast sausage, stirring frequently, until browned.
2. In a bowl, mix the flaxseed, almond flour, onion powder, garlic powder and sage together.
3. Add the eggs and cheese to the bowl, and mix.
4. Add this mixture to the sausage.
5. Line a casserole dish with parchment paper, and pour in the casserole mix. Drizzle the 2 tbsp. of syrup on top.
6. Bake at 350°F for about 45-55 minutes and cool.

Nutrition: calories 480 – Fat 41.2 – Carbs 3 - Protein 22.7

5. QUICK KETO SCRAMBLE

Prep.Time: 5 min - **Cooking Time:** 10 min -
Servings: 1

Ingredients:

- ✓ 3 eggs, whisked
- ✓ 4 baby bella mushrooms
- ✓ ¼ cup red bell peppers
- ✓ ½ cup spinach
- ✓ 2 slices deli ham
- ✓ 1 tbsp. coconut oil
- ✓ Salt and pepper

Directions:

1. Mince the vegetables and the ham.
2. Brown them in a frying pan with melted butter.
3. Add the eggs and seasonings, and scramble the eggs until cooked through.

Nutrition: calories 350 – Fat 30– Carbs 5 - Protein 20

6. KETO GREEN SMOOTHIE

Prep.Time: 5 min - **Servings:** 1

Ingredients:

- ✓ 1½ cups almond milk
- ✓ 1 oz. spinach
- ✓ ⅓ cup cucumber, diced
- ✓ ⅓ cup celery, diced
- ✓ ½ cup avocado, diced
- ✓ 1 tbsp. coconut oil
- ✓ Liquid stevia
- ✓ ¼ cup protein powder

Directions:

1. Blend the almond milk and spinach in a blender.
2. Make room for the rest of the ingredients, and blend again until a smooth consistency is achieved

Nutrition: calories 370 – Fat 24 - Carbs 5 - Protein 27

7. KETO CREPES WITH BLUEBERRIES

Prep.Time: 10 min - **Cooking Time:** 10 min -
Servings: 6

Ingredients:

- ✓ 2 oz. cream cheese
- ✓ 2 eggs
- ✓ 10 drops liquid stevia
- ✓ ¼ tsp. cinnamon
- ✓ ¼ tsp. baking soda
- ✓ ⅛ tsp. salt
  For the Filling:
- ✓ 4 oz. cream cheese
- ✓ ½ tsp. vanilla extract
- ✓ 2 tsp. powdered erythritol
- ✓ ½ cup blueberries

Directions:

1. In a bowl, mix the cream cheese and eggs with an electric hand mixer until smooth.
2. Add the stevia, cinnamon, baking soda and salt, and mix.
3. Add butter or coconut oil in a nonstick pan, and heat over medium. Pour in some batter – to make a very thin layer - and cook for 3 minutes. Flip the crepe, cook for a further minute, and remove.
4. Make the filling: combine the cream cheese, vanilla extract and powdered erythritol, and stir with the electric mixer until creamy.

5. Add the filling, cinnamon and blueberries to your crepes and either fold or roll them up

Nutrition: calories 400 – Fat 35– Carbs 6 - Protein 15

8. BREAKFAST BURGERS

Prep.Time: 15 min - **Cooking Time:** 25 min - **Servings**: 2

Ingredients:
- ✓ 4 oz. sausage
- ✓ 2 oz. pepper jack cheese
- ✓ 4 slices bacon
- ✓ 2 eggs
- ✓ 1 tbsp. butter
- ✓ 1 tbsp. peanut butter powder
- ✓ Salt and pepper

Directions:

1. Bake the bacon on a cooking sheet at 400°F for 20-25 minutes.
2. small bowl.
3. Form 2 patties from the sausage, and cook them until Combine the butter and peanut butter powder in a
4. well done.
5. Add cheese, and cover with a lid so that it melts. Remove from the pan.
6. Cook the egg and set atop the burger along with the peanut butter mix and bacon slices

Nutrition: calories 652 – Fat 55 - Carbs 3 - Protein 30

9. VERSATILE OOPSIE ROLLS

Prep.Time: 20 min - **Cooking Time:** 40 minutes - **Servings**: 6

Ingredients:

- ✓ Cooking spray
- ✓ 6 oz. cream cheese, cold and cubed
- ✓ 6 eggs
- ✓ ¼ tsp. cream of tartar
- ✓ ¼ tsp. salt

Directions:

1. Separate the egg whites and yolks. Whisk the whites with an electric hand mixer until
2. they are foamy.
3. Add cream of tartar, and keep mixing until they start to form stiff peaks.
4. In another bowl, mix the egg yolks with cream cheese until smooth, and then carefully fold in the white egg mixture.
5. Place the batter on a cookie sheet with parchment paper.
6. Bake for about 30-40 minutes and cool

Nutrition: calories 45 – Fat 4- Protein 2.5

10. ITALIAN SAUSAGE AND EGG SCRAMBLE

Prep.Time: 20 min - **Cooking Time:**60 min -
Servings:1

Ingredients:

- ✓ 1 cup red bell pepper, chopped
- ✓ 1 cup onion, chopped
- ✓ 4 eggs
- ✓ 3 spicy Italian chicken sausages
- ✓ ¼ cup mozzarella cheese, shredded
- ✓ 1 tsp. cayenne pepper powder
- ✓ Salt

Directions:

1. Place the chopped red bell peppers and onion into a skillet. Sauté until the onion starts to turn transparent, and then add the chicken sausage (chopped into small pieces).
2. Sauté just long enough to heat the sausage.
3. Add the eggs and mozzarella cheese, and mix with a spatula.
4. Scramble for a further 3-4 minutes, or until the mixture has finished cooking.
5. Add the cayenne pepper and salt to taste.

Nutrition: calories 750 – Fat 40 – Carbs 17 - Protein 75

11. CALIFORNIA STYLE OMELET

Prep.Time: 5 min - **Cooking Time:** 5 min - **Servings:** 1

Ingredients:

- ✓ 2 eggs
- ✓ 2 bacon slices, cooked and chopped
- ✓ 1 oz. deli cut chicken
- ✓ ¼ avocado
- ✓ 1 tomato
- ✓ 1 tbsp. mayonnaise
- ✓ 1 tbsp. mustard

Directions:

1. Beat the eggs and pour into a hot pan. Begin to scramble and season.
2. When eggs are halfway cooked, add the chicken, bacon, sliced avocado, and tomato.
3. Combine the mayo and mustard as well and drizzle inside.
4. Fold the omelet. Cook for 5 minutes or until heated through.

Nutrition: calories 417 – Fat 35– Carbs 5 - Protein 2

12. PEANUT BUTTER MUFFINS WITH CHOCOLATE CHIPS

Prep.Time: 10 min **Cooking Time**: 15 min - **Servings:** 2

Ingredients:

- ✓ ½ cup erythritol
- ✓ 1 cup almond flour
- ✓ 1 tbsp. baking powder
- ✓ ⅓ cup almond milk
- ✓ ⅓ cup peanut butter
- ✓ 2 eggs
- ✓ ½ cup sugar-free chocolate chips
- ✓ Salt

Directions:

1. Mix the erythritol, almond flour, and baking powder in a bowl and whisk.
2. Add the peanut butter and almond milk, and stir.
3. Add in the first egg and combine well. Add the second and combine well.
4. Fold in the chocolate chips.
5. Place the muffins in a muffin tin (of 6 cups) and bake them on 350°F for 15 minutes and cool.

Nutrition: calories 527 – Fat 40 - Carbs 4.3 - Protein 14

13. KETO BANANA PANCAKE

Prep.Time: 10 min - **Cooking Time:** 10 min - **Servings:** 4

Ingredients:

- ✓ 2 eggs
- ✓ 1 banana
- ✓ 2 tbsp. cashew nuts, ground
- ✓ ¼ tsp. cinnamon
- ✓ ¼ tsp. ground cloves
- ✓ 1 tbsp. extra virgin coconut oil
  For the Topping:
- ✓ 3 tbsp. coconut cream
- ✓ ¼ tsp. cinnamon

Directions:

1. Whisk the eggs in a small bowl.
2. In another bowl, mash the bananas with cinnamon, ground cashew nuts and ground cloves. Add the eggs to the mixture and combine well.
3. Grease a pan, heat, and make the pancakes by pouring enough batter to make a hand-size pancake. Flip when the edges are browned and the top begins to bubble.
4. When cooked, remove and top with the coconut cream and cinnamon.

Nutrition: calories 585 – Fat 45 – Carbs 27 - Protein 20

14. KETO FRENCH TOAST

Prep.Time: 15 min - **Cooking Time:** 45 min - **Servings:** 2

Ingredients:

- ✓ 14 eggs, separated
- ✓ 1 cup whey protein
- ✓ 4 oz. cream cheese, softened
- ✓ 1 cup unsweetened almond milk
- ✓ 1 tsp. vanilla
- ✓ 1 tsp. cinnamon
- ✓ ½ cup butter
- ✓ ½ cup Granulated sweetener of your choice

Directions:

1. Make the bread by mixing 12 egg whites for about 10 minutes, or until stiff peaks form. Add whey protein stirring gently, and fold in the cream cheese.
2. Grease two bread pans and pour the batter in them. Bake for about 40-45 minutes at 325°F. Remove and let them cool. Slice them to desired thickness after they have cooled completely.
3. Combine 2 eggs in a bowl, ½ cup unsweetened almond milk, vanilla and cinnamon. Dip the bread slices in the mixture.
4. Place the bread onto a skillet and grill until lightly browned on both sides. Repeat with the rest.

5. Make the sauce: place the butter in a saucepan in high heat. When it comes to a boil, and begins to brown, add the sweetener and the other ½ cup almond milk to the pan. Stir quickly to combine, then let cool in the pan for a couple minutes before pouring into a recipient. Top the toast with it

Nutrition: calories 125 – Fat 15– Carbs 0.7 - Protein 6.5

KETO SIDES RECIPES

1. MACADAMIA NUT FATTY TUNA SALAD

Prep.Time: 10 min - **Servings:** 1

Ingredients:

- 1-5 oz can Safe Catch Albacore Tuna
- 1 tbsp. Primal Kitchen mayo
- 1 tbsp. Dijon mustard (sugar free)
- 1/4 cup halved macadamia nuts
- 1 stalk green onion
- 1 tsp. sesame oil
- 9 slices cucumber
- Salt
- Pepper

Directions:

1. Open and drain tuna. Flake tuna into a bowl.
2. Add in the mayo, mustard, sesame oil, salt and pepper. Mix well.
3. Rough chop the macadamia nuts and add them to the bowl.
4. Slice the green onion and add it to the bowl.
5. Mix well.
6. Slice a firm cucumber into 9 thin rounds. Use it to scoop up tuna salad

2. ONE MINUTE KETO MAYO

Prep.Time: 10 min

Ingredients:

- 3 large egg yolks
- 1 tsp. mustard
- 1 tsp. apple cider vinegar
- 1/4 tsp. sea salt
- 1/4 tsp. black pepper
- 1 tsp. dried herb blend
- 1/2 cup olive oil

Directions:

1. Combine all of the ingredients in a large mason jar or measuring cup.
2. Insert immersion blender (stick blender) and blend until thick and creamy

KETO LUNCH RECIPES

1. KETO FLAT BREAD

Prep.Time: 10 min - **Cooking Time:** 15 min - **Servings:** 8

Ingredients:

For the Crust:
- ✓ 2 cups half-and-half grated mozzarella cheese
- ✓ 2 tbsp. cream cheese
- ✓ ¾ cup almond flour
- ✓ ½ tsp. sea salt
- ✓ ⅛ tsp. dried thyme

For the Topping:
- ✓ 1 cup grated Mexican cheese
- ✓ ½ red onion, small and sliced
- ✓ 4 oz. low carbohydrate sliced ham, cut
- ✓ ¼ medium apple, unpeeled and sliced
- ✓ ⅛ tsp. thyme, dried
- ✓ Salt and pepper

Directions:

1. Fill a saucepan with a little water and bring to the boil, then turn the heat to low. Place the saucepan inside a metal mixing bowl to form a double boiler, and add the mozzarella cheese, cream cheese, almond flour, thyme and salt. Stir with a spatula.
2. Cook until the cheese melts, and mix the ingredients into a dough. Pour some onto a 12-inch pizza tray covered with parchment paper. Roll the dough into a ball and place onto the center of the parchment paper. Pat into a disc shape to cover the pan.

3. Place the dough and the parchment paper on the pizza pan, poking holes throughout the dough with a fork, and bake for 6-8 minutes at 425°F. Remove.
4. Spread the toppings over the flatbread, along with the cheese, onion, apple and the ham. Cover with more cheese. Season with thyme, salt and pepper.
5. Bake again at 350°F for 5-7 minutes. Remove once the cheese begins to brown. Let cool before slicing.

Nutrition: calories 257 - Fat 22 - Carbs 5 - Protein 18

2. KETO SAUSAGE AND PEPPER SOUP

Prep.Time: 10 min -**Cooking Time**: 30 min - **Servings:** 6

Ingredients:

- ✓ 30 oz. pork sausage
- ✓ 1 tbsp. olive oil
- ✓ 10 oz. raw spinach
- ✓ 1 medium green bell pepper
- ✓ 1 can tomatoes with jalapeños
- ✓ 4 cups beef stock
- ✓ 1 tbsp. onion powder
- ✓ 1 tbsp. chili powder
- ✓ 1 tsp. cumin garlic powder
- ✓ 1 tsp. Italian seasoning
- ✓ Salt

Directions:

1. In a large pot, heat the olive oil over a medium heat until hot and cook the sausage. Stir.
2. Chop the green pepper and add to the pot. Stir well. Season with salt and pepper. Add the tomatoes and jalapeños. Stir.
3. Add the spinach on top and cover the pot. When it is wilted, incorporate spices and broth and combine.
4. Cover the pot again and let cook for about 30 minutes (heat medium-low). When it is done, remove the lid and let the soup simmer for around 10 minutes

Nutrition: calories 525 - Fat 45 - Carbs 4 - Protein 28

3. ZUCCHINI BOATS

Prep.Time: 15 min - **Cooking Time:** 30 minutes -
Servings: 1

Ingredients:

- ✓ 2 large zucchini
- ✓ 2 tbsp. butter
- ✓ 3 oz. shredded cheddar cheese
- ✓ 1 cup broccoli
- ✓ 6 oz. shredded rotisserie chicken
- ✓ 1 stalk green onion
- ✓ 2 tbsp. sour cream
- ✓ Salt and pepper

Directions:

1. Cut the zucchini in half lengthwise, scooping out the core until you are left with a boat shape.
2. Into each zucchini pour a little melted butter, season and place into the oven at 400°F, baking for about 18 minutes.
3. In a bowl, combine the chicken, broccoli and sour cream.
4. Place the chicken mixture inside the hollowed zucchinis.
5. Top with cheddar cheese and bake for an additional 10-15 minutes.

Nutrition: calories 480 - Fat 35 - Carbs 5- Protein 28

4. ORIGINAL SQUASH LASAGNA

Prep.Time: 10 min -**Cooking Time:** 1 hour and 30 minutes- **Servings**: 12

Ingredients:
- ✓ 1 lb. spaghetti squash
- ✓ 3 lb. ground beef
- ✓ 30 slices mozzarella cheese
- ✓ 1 large jar marinara sauce
- ✓ 32 oz. whole milk ricotta cheese

Directions:
1. Cut the spaghetti squash in two halves, placing them face down onto a baking dish. Add a half inch or so of water. Bake for 45 minutes. When finished, carefully pull out the meat of the squash.
2. In a frying pan, cook the ground beef the meat in a pan and add marinara sauce.
3. In a greased baking pan, place a layer of spaghetti squash, cover with the meat sauce, mozzarella and ricotta. Repeat until the pan is full.
4. Bake for 35 minutes at 375°F..

Nutrition: calories 710 - Fat 60 - Carbs 17 - Protein 45

5. CAULIFLOWER SOUP WITH BACON AND CHEDDAR

Prep.Time: 20 min - **Cooking Time:** 1 hour - **Servings:** 6

Ingredients:

- ✓ 1 head of cauliflower
- ✓ 2 tbsp. olive oil
- ✓ 1 medium onion, diced
- ✓ 4 slices bacon
- ✓ 1 tbsp. minced garlic
- ✓ 1 tsp. thyme
- ✓ 12 oz. aged cheddar
- ✓ 1 oz. parmesan cheese
- ✓ 3 cups chicken broth
- ✓ ¼ cup heavy cream

Directions:

1. Chop the cauliflower, and place on a foil-lined baking sheet. Sprinkle olive oil and season it with salt and pepper. Bake for 35 minutes at 375°F.
2. In a pot, cook the bacon until crispy. Add diced onion and fry it in the bacon grease. When it is tender, add the garlic and the thyme, and cook for 1 minute or less.
3. Incorporate the chicken broth and cauliflower, and simmer, covered, for 20 minutes.
4. Once time is up, blend the ingredients in a food processor or blender until smooth. Place back into the pot. Add the cheddar

and the parmesan cheese, and stir until melted.
5. Finally, add the bacon and the double cream, and mix well. If needed, simmer for 10 minutes more, or until heated

Nutrition: calories 340- Fat 26 - Carbs 10 - Protein 20

6. CHILI SOUP

Prep.Time: 20 min - Cooking Time: 6 hour- **Servings:** 8

Ingredients:

- ✓ 2 tbsp. butter, unsalted
- ✓ 2 onions
- ✓ 1 pepper
- ✓ 8 chicken thighs (boneless)
- ✓ 8 slices of bacon
- ✓ 1 cup chicken stock
- ✓ ¼ cup unsweetened coconut milk
- ✓ 3 tbsp. tomato paste
- ✓ 1 tsp. thyme
- ✓ 1 tsp. salt
- ✓ 1 tsp. pepper
- ✓ 1 tbsp. garlic, minced
- ✓ 1 tbsp. coconut flour
- ✓ 3 tbsp. lemon juice

Directions:

1. Place the butter in the center of the Crock-Pot.
2. Slice the onion and pepper, and add to the Crock-Pot. Then add the chicken thighs. Top with the bacon slices.
3. Season with salt, pepper, minced garlic, and coconut flour. Add the lemon juice, chicken stocks, coconut milk and tomato paste.
4. Cook on low for 6 hours. When it is done, stir and serve

Nutrition: calories 395 - Fat 20- Carbs 8 - Protein 40

7. KETO CASSEROLE WITH CHICKEN AND BACON

Prep.Time: 15 min - **Cooking Time:** 40 minutes - **Servings:** 12

Ingredients:

- ✓ 16 oz. frozen cauliflower
- ✓ 7 slices bacon
- ✓ 8 oz. shredded cheddar cheese
- ✓ 16 oz. cream cheese, softened
- ✓ Paprika

Directions:

1. In the oven, cook the bacon at 400°F for 15 minutes.
2. Meanwhile, dice the chicken and cook in a frying pan. Remove from pan.
3. Brown the sausage. Once it is done, transfer it to the same bowl as the chicken.
4. Chop the onion and celery, and cook them in the remaining sausage grease until translucent.
5. Defrost the cauliflower, and cut the florets into smaller pieces.
6. In a large bowl, add all the ingredients and mix well. Add the cream cheese and mix well.
7. In large pan, place the mixture and sprinkle the paprika.
8. Bake at 350°F for 30 minutes, covered with a foil. Uncover and cook for an additional 10 minutes.

Nutrition: calories 600 - Fat 41 - Carbs 6- Protein 53

8 ASIAN SALAD

Prep.Time: 15 min - **Cooking Time:**35 minutes - **Servings**: 1

Ingredients:

- ✓ 1 packet shirataki noodles
- ✓ 2 tbsp. coconut oil
- ✓ 1 cucumber
- ✓ 1 spring onion
- ✓ ¼ tbsp. red pepper flakes
- ✓ 1 tbsp. sesame oil
- ✓ 1 tbsp. rice vinegar
- ✓ 1 tsp. sesame seeds
- ✓ Salt and pepper

Directions:

1. Wash the shirataki noodles. Strain off all the excess water. Let them dry on a paper towel.
    i. In a pan, heat the coconut oil over a medium-high, and fry the noodles for 5-7 minutes. Remove and set on a paper towel to cool.
2. Peel and slice the cucumber. Arrange on a plate, and add the rest of the ingredients, sprinkling over the cucumber. Let chill for 30 minutes in the fridge.
3. Top with fried shirataki noodles.

Nutrition: calories 418 - Fat 45- Carbs 8 - Protein 3

9. MEXICAN-STYLE CASSEROLE WITH SPINACH

Prep.Time: 15 min - **Cooking Time:** 40 minutes - **Servings:** 12

Ingredients:

- ✓ 1 green pepper
- ✓ 1 onion
- ✓ 20 oz. drained spinach
- ✓ 2 lb. ground pork
- ✓ 2 cans drained diced tomatoes with green chilies
- ✓ 10 tbsp. sour cream
- ✓ 8 oz. mozzarella cheese, shredded
- ✓ 16 oz. cream cheese
- ✓ 4 tsp. taco seasoning
- ✓ Jalapeños, sliced

Directions:

1. Chop pepper and onion and cook them until translucent. Optional: add diced jalapeños.
2. Place the pepper and onion into a bowl.
3. Cook the spinach by wilting it in a frying pan with a little olive oil. When it is done, add it to the bowl.
4. Cook the ground pork until browned. Season with taco seasoning.
5. Add the diced tomato to the bowl, and incorporate the sour cream, mozzarella and cream cheese. Pour the mixture into a baking dish, and bake at 350°F for 40 minutes.

Nutrition: calories 400 - Fat 30 - Carbs 10- Protein 25

10. BBQ CHICKEN SOUP

Prep.Time: 20 min - **Cooking Time:** 50 min - **Servings**: 4

Ingredients:

- ✓ 3 medium chicken thighs
- ✓ 2 tsp. chili seasoning
- ✓ 2 tbsp. olive oil
- ✓ 1½ cups chicken broth
- ✓ 1½ cups beef broth
- ✓ BBQ sauce
- ✓ ¼ cup reduced sugar ketchup
- ✓ ¼ cup tomato paste
- ✓ 2 tbsp. Dijon mustard
- ✓ 1 tbsp. soy sauce
- ✓ 1 tbsp. hot sauce
- ✓ 2½ tsp. liquid smoke
- ✓ 1 tsp. Worcestershire sauce
- ✓ 1½ tsp. garlic powder
- ✓ 1 tsp. onion powder
- ✓ 1 tsp. chili powder
- ✓ 1 tsp. red chili flakes
- ✓ 1 tsp. cumin
- ✓ ¼ cup butter
- ✓ Salt and pepper

Directions:

1. Take the chicken thighs and de-bone. Reserve the bones. Season with favorite chili seasoning. Bake for 50 minutes at 400°F on a baking tray with foil.
2. In a pot, place olive oil and set on medium high heat. Once it is hot, add the chicken

bones. Cook them for 5 minutes and add the broth. Season with salt and pepper.
3. When chicken is done, take off the skin. Incorporate the fat from the chicken into the broth and stir.
4. Make the BBQ Sauce: combine all the already mentioned ingredients for the sauce. Add it to the pot and stir. Let it simmer 20-30 minutes.
5. Emulsify all the fats and liquid together with an immersion blender. Shred the chicken and incorporate into the soup. Cook for 10-20 minutes more.

Nutrition: calories 395 - Fat 19.5 - Fiber 3.5 - Carbs 12.5 - Protein 42

11. ALMOND PIZZA

Prep.Time: 10 min - **Cooking Time:** 15 min - **Servings:** 4

Ingredients:

- ¾ cup almond meal
- 1½ tsp. baking powder
- 1½ tsp. granulated sweetener
- ½ tsp. oregano
- ¼ tsp. thyme
- ½ tsp. garlic powder
- 2 eggs
- 5 tbsp. butter
- ½ cup alfredo sauce
- 4 oz. cheddar cheese

Directions:

1. Mix the dry ingredients together in a large bowl.
2. Take the eggs (at room temperature) and add to the dry mixture.
3. Melt the butter and incorporate.
4. On a greased pizza pan, spread the crust and pre-cook at 350°F for about 7 minutes.
5. Remove from the oven, and spread the Alfredo Sauce and cheddar cheese on top. Let cook for 5 minutes more.

Nutrition: calories 460 - Fat 45 - Carbs 5 - Protein 15

12. KETO ENCHILADA SOUP

Prep.Time: 20 min - Cooking Time: 45 min- **Servings:** 4

Ingredients:

- ✓ 3 tbsp. olive oil
- ✓ 3 diced celery stalks
- ✓ 1 medium diced red bell pepper
- ✓ 2 tsp. minced garlic
- ✓ 1 cup diced tomatoes
- ✓ 2 tsp. cumin
- ✓ 1 tsp. oregano
- ✓ 1 tsp. chili powder
- ✓ ½ tsp. cayenne pepper
- ✓ ½ cup chopped cilantro
- ✓ 4 cups chicken broth
- ✓ 8 oz. cream cheese
- ✓ 6 oz. shredded chicken
- ✓ Juice of ½ a lime

Directions:

1. In a hot pan with olive oil, sauté the celery and pepper. When the celery starts to become tender, add the tomatoes and cook for 2-3 minutes longer.
2. Incorporate the spices. Add the chicken broth and cilantro, letting it boil. Reduce to a low heat, and simmer for about 20 minutes.
3. Add the cheese and boil again. Reduce to a low heat and simmer for 25 minutes more.
4. Add the shredded chicken with the lime juice. Stir.
5. Season with cilantro and serve.

Nutrition: calories 345 - Fat 31 - Carbs 6.3 - Protein 13

13. KETO PORK STEW

Prep.Time: 25 min - **Cooking Time:** 4/10 hours -
Servings: 4

Ingredients:

- ✓ 1 lb. pork shoulder, cooked and sliced
- ✓ 2 tsp. chili powder
- ✓ 2 tsp. cumin
- ✓ 1 tsp. garlic, minced
- ✓ ½ tsp. salt
- ✓ ½ tsp. pepper
- ✓ 1 tsp. paprika
- ✓ 1 tsp. oregano
- ✓ ¼ tsp. cinnamon
- ✓ 2 bay leaves
- ✓ 6 oz. button mushrooms
- ✓ ½ jalapeño, sliced
- ✓ ½ onion, medium
- ✓ ½ sliced green bell pepper
- ✓ ½ sliced red bell pepper
- ✓ Juice of ½ a lime
- ✓ 2 cups gelatinous bone broth
- ✓ 2 cups chicken broth
- ✓ ½ cup strong coffee
- ✓ ¼ cup tomato paste

Directions:

1. Dice the vegetables, and sauté them in a pan lined with olive oil over high heat. Remove from heat when browned.

2. Chop pork and put into a slow cooker with mushrooms, bone broth, chicken broth and coffee.
3. Incorporate spices and vegetables as well and mix. Place the lid. Cook for 4-10 hours on low.

Nutrition: calories 385 - Fat 29- Carbs 6.4- Protein 20

14. KETO CHICKEN TIKKA MASALA

Prep.Time: 10 min - **Cooking Time**: 3/6 hours –
Servings: 5

Ingredients:

- ✓ 1 lb. chicken thighs (boneless/skinless)
- ✓ 2 tbsp. olive oil
- ✓ 2 tsp. onion powder
- ✓ 3 minced garlic cloves
- ✓ 1 inch grated ginger root
- ✓ 3 tbsp. tomato paste
- ✓ 5 tsp. garam masala
- ✓
- ✓ 2 tsp. smoked paprika
- ✓ 4 tsp. kosher salt
- ✓ 10 oz. diced tomatoes (can)
- ✓ 1 cup heavy cream
- ✓ 1 cup coconut milk
- ✓ Fresh chopped cilantro
- ✓ 1 tsp. guar gum

Directions:

1. De-bone the chicken thighs. Chop the chicken into bite-sized pieces.
2. In a slow cooker, add the chicken and grate the ginger on top. In another bowl, mix the tomato paste and canned tomatoes with the rest of the dry spices. Add ½ cup coconut milk and stir. Add to the slow cooker.
3. Cook on low for 6 hours or on high for 3 hours.

4. Once finished, add the remaining coconut milk, double cream, and guar gum. Mix

Nutrition: calories 495 - Fat 43 - Carbs 5 - Protein 25

15. BACON WRAP

Prep.Time: 10 min - **Cooking Time:** 5 min - **Servings:** 4

Ingredients:

- ✓ 16 oz. beef
- ✓ Montreal steak seasoning
- ✓ 4 bacon slices Salt and pepper

Directions:

1. Cut the beef into cubes   and season it.
2. Cut the bacon slices in four.
3. Wrap the beef with the bacon, and pierce with a toothpick. Repeat 2 or 3 times. Fry for 3 minutes.

Nutrition: calories 217 - Fat 10 – Carbs 0 - Protein 30

16. SPAGHETTI SQUASH WITH MEAT SAUCE

Prep.Time: 20 min - Cooking Time: 45 min -**Servings:** 8

Ingredients:

- ✓ 2 spaghetti squashes
- ✓ 2 lb. ground beef
- ✓ 33-oz. jar of spaghetti sauce
- ✓ 1 tbsp. minced garlic
- ✓ 1 tbsp. Italian seasoning
- ✓ Parmesan cheese

Directions:

1. Cut the spaghetti squash in half and scrape out the guts. Cook the remaining shell and meat in a glass container partially filled with water at 375°F for 45 minutes or until soft.
2. Brown some beef on the stove. Add the seasonings, the sauce, and mix. Heat through.
3. Carefully remove the cooked spaghetti squash from the oven, and use a fork to create the spaghetti. Serve with the sauce.

Nutrition: calories 170 - Fat 15 - Carbs 12- Protein 11

17. HAM AND CHEESE KETO STROMBOLI

Prep.Time: 20 min - **Cooking Time:** 20 minutes - **Servings:** 4

Ingredients:

- ✓ 1 1/4 cups Mozzarella
- ✓ Cheese, shredded
- ✓ 4 tbsp. Almond Flour
- ✓ 3 tbsp. Coconut Flour
- ✓ 1 large Egg
- ✓ 1 tsp. Italian Seasoning
- ✓ 4 oz. Ham
- ✓ 3.5 oz. Cheddar Cheese
- ✓ Salt and Pepper to Taste

Directions:

1. Preheat your oven to 400F and in a microwave or toaster oven, melt your mozzarella cheese. About 1 minute in the microwave, and 10 second intervals afterward, or about 10 minutes in an oven, stirring occasionally.
2. Combine almond and coconut flour, as well as your seasonings in a mixing bowl. I used salt, pepper and an Italian blend seasoning.
3. When the mozzarella is melted, place that into your flour mixture and begin working it in.
4. After about a minute, when the cheese has had a chance to cool down a bit, add in your egg and combine everything

together. It helps to use two utensils here.

5. When everything is combined and you've got a moist dough, transfer it to a flat surface with some parchment paper.
6. Lay a second sheet of parchment paper over the dough ball and use a rolling pin or your hand to flatten it out.
7. Use a pizza cutter or knife to cut diagonal lines beginning from the edges of the dough to the center, leave a row of dough untouched about 4 inches wide.
8. Alternate laying ham and cheddar on that uncut stretch of dough.
9. Then lift one section of dough at a time and lay it over the top, covering your filling.
10. Then bake it for about 15-20 minutes until you see it has turned a golden brown color.

Nutrition: calories 306 - Fat 21.8 - Carbs 4.7- Protein 25.6

18. KETO MIXED GREEN SPRING SALAD

Prep.Time: 10 min - **Servings**: 1

Ingredients:

- ✓ 2 OZ. Mixed Greens
- ✓ 3 tbsp. Pine Nuts, roasted
- ✓ 2 tbsp. 5 Minute Keto Raspberry Vinaigrette
- ✓ 2 tbsp. Shaved Parmesan
- ✓ 2 slices Bacon
- ✓ Salt and Pepper to taste

Directions:

1. Cook bacon until very crisp. I let mine slightly burn on the edges to give the salad a slight addition in bitter notes in some bites.
2. Measure out your greens and set in a container that can be shaken.
3. Crumble bacon, then add the rest of the ingredients to the greens. Shake the container with a lid on to distribute the dressing and contents evenly.

Nutrition: calories 478 - Fat 37.3 - Carbs 4.3- Protein 17.1

19.PORTOBELLO PERSONAL PIZZAS

Prep.Time: 20 min **-Cooking Time:** 15 minutes -
Servings: 4

Ingredients:

- ✓ 4 large Portobello Mushroom
- ✓ Caps
- ✓ 1 medium Vine Tomato
- ✓ 4 oz. Fresh Mozzarella
- ✓ Cheese
- ✓ 1/4 cup Fresh Chopped Basil
- ✓ 6 tbsp. Olive Oil
- ✓ 20 slices Pepperoni
- ✓ Salt and Pepper to Taste

Directions:

1. Get your 4 portobello mushrooms ready.
2. Scrape out all of the innards of the mushroom. Then dig into the flesh and get the mushroom about 1cm thick.
3. Set the oven to broil on high and rub the insides of each mushroom with just under 1 tbsp. Olive Oil. You should use 3 tbsp. Olive Oil between the 4 mushrooms. Season with salt and pepper to taste.
4. Broil the mushroom for about 4-5 minutes.
5. Flip the mushrooms over and rub again with 3 tbsp. Olive Oil. Season with salt and pepper to taste. Broil the mushrooms with the other side facing up for about 3-4 minutes longer.

6. Slice a tomato thin, about 12-16 slices in total. Chop 1/4 cup basil into strips.
7. Lay the tomato and basil into each mushroom. depending on how many slices of tomato, you will put 3-4 slices in each mushroom. About 1 tbsp. of basil on top of each mushroom also.
8. Lay 5 slices of pepperoni onto each mushroom and top with fresh cubed mozzarella cheese (1 oz per mushroom).

Broil again for 2-4 minutes, or until cheese is melted and starts to brown

Nutrition: calories 321 - Fat 31- Carbs 2.8- Protein 8.5

KETO DINNER RECIPES

1. LOW CARB CHICKEN NUGGETS

Prep.Time: 15 min - **Cooking Time:** 20 min - **Servings: 4**

Ingredients:

For the Nuggets:
- ✓ 24 oz. chicken thighs
- ✓ 1 egg

For the Crust:
- ✓ 1½ oz. pork rinds
- ✓ ¼ cup flax meal
- ✓ ¼ cup almond meal
- ✓ Zest of 1 lime
- ✓ ⅛ tsp. garlic powder
- ✓ ¼ tsp. paprika
- ✓ ¼ tsp. chili powder
- ✓ ⅛ tsp. onion powder
- ✓ ⅛ tsp. cayenne pepper
- ✓ ¼ tsp. salt
- ✓ ¼ tsp. pepper

For the Sauce:
- ✓ ½ cup mayonnaise
- ✓ ½ avocado
- ✓ ¼ tsp. garlic powder
- ✓ 1 tbsp. lime juice
- ✓ ⅛ tsp. cumin
- ✓ ½ tsp. red chili flakes

Directions:

1. Dry the chicken and cut into bite-size pieces.
2. Put all the crust ingredients into a food processor and mix.

3. In a bowl place the crumbs and a whisked egg in a different one. Dip the chicken into the egg, the crust and then lay on a greased baking sheet. Bake for 15-20 minutes at 400°F.
4. To make the sauce, just mix all the sauce ingredients together.

Nutrition: calories 615 - Fat 53 - Carbs 2- Protein 39

2. KETO PARMESAN CHICKEN

Prep.Time: 20 min - **Cooking Time:** 10 min - **Servings:**4

Ingredients:

For the Chicken:
- ✓ 3 chicken breasts
- ✓ 1 cup mozzarella cheese
- ✓ Salt and pepper

For the Coating:
- ✓ 2½ oz. pork rinds
- ✓ ¼ cup flaxseed meal
- ✓ ½ cup parmesan cheese
- ✓ 1 tsp. oregano
- ✓ ½ tsp. salt
- ✓ ½ tsp. pepper
- ✓ ¼ tsp. red pepper flakes
- ✓ ½ tsp. garlic
- ✓ 2 tsp. paprika
- ✓ 1 egg
- ✓ 1½ tsp. chicken broth

The Sauce
- ✓ ¼ cup olive oil
- ✓ 1 cup tomato sauce
- ✓ ½ tsp. garlic
- ✓ ½ tsp. oregano
- ✓ Salt and pepper

Directions:

1. In a food processor, grind up the pork rinds, parmesan cheese and spices. Slice

the chicken breasts into thirds, and season them with salt and pepper.
2. In another bowl, make the coating: whisk eggs and add the chicken broth.
3. Begin to make the sauce by combining all the sauce ingredients in a saucepan and whisking. Let simmer for 20 minutes.
4. Bread the chicken slices: dip them into the egg mixture and then into the pork rind coating. Place on a piece of foil.
5. In a pan, heat a few tbsp. of olive oil and fry the chicken. Place the fried chicken into a casserole dish, cover with sauce and cheese. Bake for 10 minutes at 400°F.

Nutrition: calories 646- Fat 47 - Carbs 5- Protein 49

3. CHEDDAR BISCUITS

Prep.Time: 10 min - **Cooking Time:** 10 min - **Servings:** 1

Ingredients:

- ✓ 2 cups Carbquik
- ✓ 2 oz. unsalted butter, cold
- ✓ 4 oz. shredded cheddar cheese
- ✓ ½ tsp. garlic powder
- ✓ ½ tsp. salt
- ✓ ¼ cup heavy cream
- ✓ ¼ cup water

Directions:

1. In a bowl, mix Carbquik and add the cold butter. Cut in the pieces of butter until the mixture has little balls of butter and flour about the size of peas. Add the cheese, garlic powder and salt and combine together.
2. Add the heavy cream and water. Mix until a dough forms. Separate them into 6 pieces and place on a greased sheet. Bake them at 450°F for about 8-10 minutes.

Nutrition: **calories 45 - Fat 4 - Carbs 2.5 - Protein 1.6**

4. KETO BROCCOLI SOUP

Prep.Time: 10 min - **Cooking Time:** 10 min - **Servings: 4**

Ingredients:

- ✓ 1 head broccoli
- ✓ ¼ cup heavy cream
- ✓ ¼ cup cream cheese
- ✓ ¼ cup sour cream
- ✓ ¼ cup almond milk
- ✓ 4 oz. cheddar cheese
- ✓ ½ onion
- ✓ ½ chicken bouillon cube

Directions:

1. Remove the florets from the broccoli. Steam them on the stove.
2. Put the florets into a blender and add the rest of the ingredients. Blend until the mixture reaches the desired consistency.
3. Pour into a pot and simmer until heated (10 minutes or so).

Nutrition: calories 270 - Fat 25 - Carbs 8 - Protein 10

5. KETO PORK CHOPS

Prep.Time: 20 min - **Servings:** 4

Ingredients:

- ✓ ½ tsp. peppercorns
- ✓ 1 medium star anise
- ✓ 1 stalk lemongrass
- ✓ 4 halved garlic cloves
- ✓ 4 pork chops (boneless)
- ✓ 1 tbsp. fish sauce
- ✓ 1 tbsp. almond flour
- ✓ 1½ tsp. soy sauce
- ✓ 1 tsp. sesame oil
- ✓ ½ tsp. five spice
- ✓ ½ tbsp. sambal chili paste
- ✓ ½ tbsp. sugar free ketchup

Directions:

1. Pulverize the peppercorn and star anise (using blender or a mortar).
2. Mix the lemongrass with garlic, fish sauce, soy sauce, sesame oil and five spice powder. Add the powdered peppercorn and star anise. Blend in a food processor until combined.
3. Set the pork on a tray and cover with the mixture on both sides. Cover the tray and marinate for 1-2 hours.
4. Lightly cover each pork chop with almond flour, and pan-fry them at a high temperature. Sear the outsides. Make sure they are done on both sides. Remove and chop into strips. Mix the sambal chili paste

and sugar-free ketchup to make the dipping sauce, and serve.

Nutrition: calories 224 - Fat 10 - Carbs 5 - Protein 35

6. CREAMY CHICKEN

Prep.Time: 10 min - **Cooking Time:** 10 min - **Servings:** 1

Ingredients:

- ✓ 5 oz. chicken breast
- ✓ 1 tbsp. olive oil
- ✓ 3 oz. mushrooms
- ✓ ¼ small onion, sliced
- ✓ ½ cup chicken broth
- ✓ ¼ cup heavy cream
- ✓ ½ tsp. dried tarragon
- ✓ 1 tsp. grain mustard
- ✓ Salt and pepper

Directions:

1. Cut the chicken into cubes, season them, and brown with olive oil. Remove and place on a plate.
2. Add mushrooms to the same pan and cook until browned. Add the onion and cook until the onion is translucent.
3. Add the chicken broth. Reduce by letting it boil for 3-5 minutes.
4. Add the rest of the ingredients and seasonings, and mix. Add the chicken, and let it simmer 3-5 more minutes.

Nutrition: calories 489 - Fat 43 - Carbs 5 - Protein 30

7. KETO THAI ZOODLES

Prep.Time: 20 min - **Cooking Time:** 10 min - **Servings:** 1

Ingredients:

- ✓ 3½ oz. chicken thighs
- ✓ ½ tsp. curry powder
- ✓ 3½ oz. zucchini
- ✓ 1 stalk spring onion
- ✓ 1 clove garlic
- ✓ 1 tsp. soy sauce
- ✓ ½ tsp. oyster sauce
- ✓ ⅛ tsp. white pepper
- ✓ 1 tbsp. butter
- ✓ 1 tbsp. coconut oil
- ✓ 1 egg
- ✓ 1⅕ oz. bean sprouts
- ✓ 1 tsp. lime juice
- ✓ Chopped red chilies
- ✓ Salt and pepper

Directions:

1. Marinate the chicken with curry powder, salt and pepper. Make the zoodles out of the zucchini by slicing it into very thin strips. Chop the onion and garlic into small pieces. Make the sauce by mixing the soy sauce, oyster sauce and white pepper.
2. Cook the chicken with the butter until they are browned and cut into bit-sized pieces.

3. In the same pan on high heat, add coconut oil and sauté the onion and the garlic. Add the egg and cook until slightly browned.
4. Add in the bean sprouts and zoodles, and mix. Pour in the sauce, add the chicken, and stir.
5. Garnish with some chopped red chillies and lemon juice.

Nutrition: calories 581 - Fat 50 - Carbs 7- Protein 26

8. KUNG PAO CHICKEN

Prep.Time: 15 min - **Cooking Time:** 15 min - **Servings:**4

Ingredients:

For the Chicken:
- ✓ 2 medium chicken thighs
- ✓ 1 tsp. ground ginger
- ✓ ¼ cup peanuts
- ✓ ½ green pepper
- ✓ 4 de-seeded red bird's eye chilies
- ✓ 2 large spring onions
- ✓ Salt and pepper

For the Sauce:
- ✓ 1 tbsp. soy sauce
- ✓ 2 tbsp. chili garlic paste
- ✓ 2 tsp. rice wine vinegar
- ✓ 1 tbsp. reduced-sugar ketchup
- ✓ ½ tsp. maple extract
- ✓ 2 tsp. sesame oil
- ✓ 10 drops liquid stevia

Directions:

1. Cut the chicken into small pieces and season with salt, pepper and ginger.
2. Cook the chicken in a pan over a medium-high heat until browned (approximately 10 minutes).
3. Make the sauce by combining all the sauce ingredients.
4. Chop the vegetables and chilies. When the chicken is done, add all the ingredients and

cook for 3-4 minutes longer. Add the sauce
and let it boil until reduced.

Nutrition: calories 360 - Fat 27.5 - Carbs 3- Protein 22

9. CHICKEN SATAY

Prep.Time: 10 min - **Servings: 3**

Ingredients:

- ✓ 1 lb. ground chicken
- ✓ 4 tbsp. soy sauce
- ✓ 3 tbsp. peanut butter
- ✓ 1 tbsp. erythritol
- ✓ 1 tbsp. rice vinegar
- ✓ 2 tsp. sesame oil
- ✓ 2 tsp. chili paste
- ✓ 1 tsp. minced garlic
- ✓ ¼ tsp. cayenne
- ✓ ¼ tsp. paprika
- ✓ ½ tsp. lime juice
- ✓ 2 chopped spring onions
- ✓ ⅓ sliced yellow pepper

Directions:

1. In a pan over a medium-high heat, put the sesame oil and sauté the ground chicken. Add the rest of the ingredients and mix well.
2. When it is cooked, add the onions and yellow pepper and mix.

Nutrition: calories 395 - Fat 24 -Carbs 4 - Protein 35

10. KETO TOTCHOS

Prep.Time: 10 min - **Cooking Time**: 5 min - **Servings:** 2

Ingredients:

- ✓ 2 servings keto tater tots
- ✓ 6 oz. ground beef
- ✓ 2 oz. shredded cheddar cheese
- ✓ 2 tbsp. sour cream
- ✓ 6 sliced black olives
- ✓ 1 tbsp. salsa
- ✓ ½ jalapeño pepper, sliced

Directions:

1. In a small casserole pan, place 9-10 keto tots and add half of the ground beef and half of the cheese. Place a second layer of tots, and add the rest of the meat and cheese.
2. Broil in the oven for 5 minutes until the cheese melts, and serve with sour cream, black olives, salsa and jalapeño.

Nutrition: calories 638 - Fat 53 – Carbs 6 - Protein 32

NOTE YOUR FAVORITE RECIPES

PAGE	NUMBER	RECIPE NAME

CPSIA information can be obtained
at www.ICGtesting.com
Printed in the USA
LVHW012315230621
690964LV00016B/1249